ZIMBABWE

Gospel and Culture pamphlets:

1. S. Wesley Ariarajah, *An Ongoing Discussion in the Ecumenical Movement*
2. Stan McKay and Janet Silman, *The First Nations of Canada*
3. Ion Bria, *Romania*
4. Noel Davies, *Wales*
5. James Massey, *Panjab*
6. Antonie Wessels, *Secularized Europe*
7. Israel Selvanayagam, *Tamilnadu*
8. Ambrose Moyo, *Zimbabwe*
9. John Pobee, *West Africa*

GOSPEL AND CULTURES PAMPHLET 8

ZIMBABWE
The Risk of Incarnation

Ambrose Moyo

WCC Publications, Geneva

Cover design: Edwin Hassink/WCC
Cover photo: A Methodist worship service near Gweru,
Zimbabwe (WCC/Peter Williams)

ISBN 2-8254-1196-5

© 1996 WCC Publications, World Council of Churches,
150 route de Ferney, 1211 Geneva 2, Switzerland

No. 8 in the Gospel and Cultures series

Printed in Switzerland

Table of Contents

vii	INTRODUCTION
1	1. GOSPEL, CULTURE AND RELIGION: DEFINING THE RELATIONSHIPS
9	2. GOSPEL, CULTURE AND CHRISTIAN MISSIONS
16	3. GOSPEL, CULTURE AND CHRISTIAN LIFE
22	4. GOSPEL AND CULTURE AND THE STATE
27	5. GOSPEL AND CULTURE IN THE AFRICAN INDEPENDENT CHURCHES
36	6. CHRIST, CULTURE AND SALVATION
47	7. THE RISK OF INCARNATION

Introduction

The proclamation of the gospel has had a significant impact on the culture and the peoples of Zimbabwe. It is estimated that today approximately 70 percent of the population is Christian.[1] The rest are mainly adherents of African traditional religions, with a small percentage of Muslims. In terms of government policy, Zimbabwe is a secular state, officially not committed to a particular religious faith or confession. But the government recognizes that most Zimbabweans are religious and is committed to guaranteeing religious freedom to all its citizens.

In practice the situation looks different. Christianity seems to occupy a special position in Zimbabwean society and might appear to be *de facto* the official religion of the state. No other religious tradition is as prominent on state-controlled radio and television. State funerals to date have been conducted according to Christian rites. To be sure, all those who have died with "hero" status since independence have been Christians — an indication of the impact of Christianity on Zimbabwe — but it is common for even non-Christians to request Christian church leaders in their communities to conduct burial ceremonies for non-Christian relatives. The gospel is seen as a blessing even to those who have died before formally accepting the Christian faith and affirming it through baptism.

A little more than a hundred years after the gospel was first preached in Zimbabwe nobody can ignore the reality of the church and the challenge of the gospel to the whole culture and religious life of the people there. Christian witness in Zimbabwe involves a dialogue between the gospel and the African cultures, including their religious beliefs and practices. At the beginning, Christianity was presented and understood as synonymous with the Euro-American cultures out of which the missionaries to Africa came. Indeed, Ian Smith, the last prime minister of Rhodesia, rejected black majority rule on the grounds that it would mean the end of what he called "a Christian civilization". The Zimbabwean nationalists rejected the perception that Christianity and

Western culture were inseparably bound together; and in defence of their human dignity, they took up arms to fight against a system which, contrary to the message of Christ as they understood it, created a gospel and culture alliance which justified a social, economic and political system that subjugated, dehumanized and impoverished other peoples and their cultures. However, they did not "throw out the baby with the bath water", but instead affirmed the gospel of Christ and pledged to support the work of the church.

Are there lessons to be learned from this Zimbabwean experience of the relationship between gospel and culture? This pamphlet is intended to contribute to the ongoing ecumenical discussion of gospel and culture by examining the interactive dynamics of this encounter as it has taken place and continues to take place in Zimbabwe. What impact has the gospel had on the peoples of Zimbabwe? In that process how have African cultures affected the African understanding of the gospel? And what does all this mean for our understanding of the relationship between gospel and culture in general?

The gospel and culture encounter in Zimbabwe has many facets. The country itself is home to a variety of African cultures, and the gospel was brought through many different and often conflicting missionary cultures. To the various denominational perspectives, both foreign and indigenous, one must also add the social, economic and political factors. What lessons does the Zimbabwean experience offer about the role of culture in the transmission and reception of the gospel? What does the gospel and culture encounter mean for Christians living in Zimbabwe today?

If the traditional approach to mission associated Christianity with the Western cultures through which the gospel reached Zimbabwe, the question today is whether there is an alternative approach to communicating the gospel. Fundamentally, this discussion is about human beings who are called to believe in Christ through the preaching of the gospel and to live out that faith on a day-to-day basis. If the gospel affects the believer's day-to-day living, what then is its relationship to culture? Can these even be separated from each other? Is it really possible to talk of a pure gospel untouched and untainted by any culture? If the symbols and images used through the ages to communicate the gospel are culturally rooted, is it possible to get to the kernel or essence of the gospel, to an aspect of it which transcends all culture? If so, what is it? And how do we get to it without going through specific cultures? This is the old issue of the "particularity" and "universality" of the gospel.

What is culture? How is it understood from a Zimbabwean perspective? How is gospel to be defined in the light of the Zimbabwean experience? What is the relationship between traditional cultures and religion in Zimbabwe? Answers to these questions should give us clues to an African perspective on the relationship between gospel and culture in Zimbabwe. In discussing gospel and culture within the context of African traditional cultures and religions in Zimbabwe, our aim is not to romanticize the African past. Zimbabwean culture today has a great deal which has continued from the past despite the efforts of the colonial powers to destroy those cultures. For many Zimbabweans the life described here is no longer meaningful; but many others want to rediscover that past and relive it. For most Zimbabweans today, I believe, the search is for a balance between the two. The focus of our discussion therefore will not be on a culture that no longer exists, but on the experience of most Zimbabweans today.

NOTE

[1] Accurate church membership statistics are difficult to obtain. This estimate is taken from the *News Sheet of the Rhodesia Catholic Bishops Conference*, no. 43, Feb. 1974; it is corroborated by the Zimbabwe Bible Society. Cf. also the statistics and projections in David B. Barrett, *World Christian Encyclopedia: A Comparative Study of Churches and Religions in the Modern World*, Nairobi, New York, London, Oxford UP, 1982.

1. Gospel, Culture and Religion: Defining the Relationships

According to Richard Niebuhr's classic definition, culture is "the total process of human activity and the total result of such activity... It comprises language, habits, ideas, beliefs, customs, social organization, inherited artifacts, technical process and values."[1] Accordingly, culture has to do with people in all aspects of their existence — social, economic, political, religious and otherwise. This means that every people is capable of producing a culture of its own and human beings can only be cultural beings, inseparable from their cultures. An address to any people is simultaneously an address to their culture.[2]

The gospel can be defined as that message which calls people to faith in Jesus Christ. In believing and identifying themselves with Christ in his death and in the hope of the resurrection to eternal life, they become a new creation, one that is truly in the image of God as was intended at the beginning of creation. The new creation, however, grows out of the old as the result of the transforming work of the gospel through the Holy Spirit. The aim of the gospel is to transform people. The transformation of people is simultaneously the transformation of their culture. The old must pass away and give way to the new (2 Cor. 5:17).

Has such a transformation taken place in the Christian communities in Zimbabwe? Has the preaching of the gospel in Zimbabwe been able to create a new culture? To respond we must look briefly at the major components of Zimbabwean traditional culture, the nature of the encounter of the gospel with it and the conflicts engendered in the attempt to create a new culture and a new people.

In African traditional thought, religion is not just another aspect of culture but something inseparable from it: a way of life which embraces all aspects of human relations. Zimbabwean traditional thought cannot conceive of a human being without religion and without participating in the life, beliefs and practices of the community. Religion and culture are as it were interchangeable. No African language of which I am aware, particularly in southern Africa, has a word equivalent to the English term "religion". The idea of such a thing, isolated from the rest of life and practised on its own, does not exist. In the holistic worldview characteristic of all of Africa, there can be no separation between the sacred and the profane, the spiritual and the material. Religion interweaves everything; hence, asking an African "What is your religion?" is like asking "What is your way of life?" or "Can you tell me something about your culture?" Culture, therefore, as understood in Zimbabwean traditional thought, which continues to dominate thinking today, is a whole way of life in which the invisible and visible worlds overlap; humanity and the whole of creation live in a world in which everything is mutually dependent.

It will be helpful at this point to give a brief survey of Shona traditional religion as representative of the traditional religions of Zimbabwe. Most African peoples have believed in a Supreme Being who is the creator and sustainer of the world. African mythology is full of episodes of interaction between that Supreme Being and the African people. The account of the migration of the Shona peoples is one of many African stories about experiences of God in mythical language. During the long journey from a place known as Guruuswa, the voice of Mwari guided the Shona through the wilderness, providing them with as much food as they needed, speaking to them through birds, bushes, caves and other natural phenomena until they reached their allotted places in Zimbabwe. Since then the voice has continued to be heard through its prophets and can be consulted to this day at one of the Matopo Hills, called Matonjeni, not far from Bulawayo.

It is particularly fascinating to consider the similarities between this story and the biblical accounts of the call of Abraham and the Exodus. God, in the Shona understanding even before the gospel was preached in Zimbabwe, was not the remote High God of the anthropologists, but one with whom they could communicate, one who could get angry and punish the people by causing drought or an epidemic, one whom the people could consult when there was a dispute regarding chieftainship, a God who could be involved in the politics of the people as well as in their social and economic lives.

Some African traditions (though I know of none in the southern Africa region) seem to have known God as existing in some kind of a trinity. Consider, for example, the following excerpt from an interview with a traditional religious leader of the Ankole of Uganda:

> Before the Europeans came to Uganda and before the white Christian missionaries came…, we had our own religion, and we knew God… so well that the missionaries added to us little… We even knew God to be some kind of eternally existing triplets: *Nyamuhanga* being the first one and being also the creator of everything, *Kazooba Nyamuhanga* being his second brother who gives light to all human beings so that they should not stumble either on the path or even in their lives… Kazooba's light penetrates the hearts of people and God sees the contents of the human hearts by Kazooba's eternal light… The third brother in the group is *Rugaba Rwa Nyamuhanga*, who takes what Nyamuhanga has created and gives it to the people as he wishes… We had it all before the missionaries came, and all they did teach us was that Nyamuhanga is God the Father, Kazooba is Jesus Christ his son, and not his brother as we thought, and Rugaba, as the divine giver, is the Holy Spirit.[3]

This is corroborated in a document by an early Roman Catholic missionary to the region, Father F. Geraud:

> They [the Bakiga people] were offering sacrifices, and after roasting the meat they would gather some of it, put it on leaves (*kiko*) and bring it to the hut dedicated to Mandwa. Then they would say: "eat, be satisfied, give to the one who gives to you, and recognize the one who gives to you, and recognize the one who refuses you. Come to me, your ears and eyes, and return to your dwelling; open my eyes to see…" They would then gather some meat not offered to Mandwa, and divide it into three parts. A man would throw up one piece saying: "This is for you, Ruhanga/Nyamuhanga (God Creator), who created me."

Then he would take another piece and say: "This is for Rugaba (the Giver), who gives me life." With the third piece of meat he would say: "This is for Kazooba (Sun/Light), who shows me the way." Sometimes they would take the three pieces of meat together and throw them up (all at once) saying: "These are yours..., *Banyinabutuka* (Landlords) Nyamuhanga, Kazooba and Rugaba." Then after the meal they would say: "Landlords eat from there, make me see, travel and return, take away from me all my enemies."[4]

These and similar accounts from other African cultures show that belief in God was a part and parcel of traditional African life before the preaching of the gospel. In traditional African societies, religion was not a matter for the individual but for the community. For one born in an African community, its religion automatically becomes one's religion. In traditional societies, belief in God is simply taken for granted and never questioned. Atheism is foreign to African thought. As children grow up they are taught certain actions that point to the existence of God.

It has been alleged that although there is a belief in one Supreme Being in most African traditional religions, that Supreme Being, after creating the universe, retired to some remote place in the heavens and remains there uninterested and unconcerned about what goes on below. This leads to the conclusion that African traditional religions do not worship the Supreme Being, but some lesser divinities or departed elders who now rule the world. This distorts and misunderstands the African traditional cultures. To understand the relationships with God and the departed elders one must understand the African kinship system.

Traditional thought does not always permit direct communication with God. In most cases this was accepted only in cases of emergency, where one was faced with danger that would result in immediate death, for example when confronted by a wild lion or leopard, or when thunder and lightning strike, or when one is in danger of drowning. Then the individual would cry directly to God for salvation. Any other serious approach to God has to be mediated by some beings that are hierarchically closer to God. These intermediaries may take the form of the *vadzimu/amadhlozi* (departed elders), as is the case among most of the so-called Bantu peoples. A clear distinction is always made between these beings and the Supreme Being. Their status is always lower than that of God, and they are often referred to as children of God or as manifestations of God.

The point I am making is that Zimbabwean traditional religions do worship the Supreme Being — and did so even before Christianity or Islam came to Zimbabwe. Usually such worship was mediated by the departed elders. The confusion arises from the fact that among most of the traditionalists prayers and sacrifices are rarely made to the Supreme Being, but to the spirit elders with whom the living communicate on a daily basis. These petitions may conclude by requesting the last person in the hierarchy to forward the petition to the Supreme Being, but since this is not always the case — and in some traditions is never the case — outsiders may get the impression that African traditionalists worship their ancestors. However, when interviewed the traditionalists will categorically deny that they worship their ancestor spirits but God through them.

Ancestor spirits are departed elders. Their role must be understood in the light of the high respect accorded to elders in traditional African societies. If, for example, one has grievously wronged one's parents, it would be considered utterly disrespectful and unacceptable to go directly to them to ask for forgiveness. One must go through some respectable elderly person to whom one would give a token to be taken to the parent. Similarly, when a young man and woman wish to marry, the prospective father-in-law must be approached by the young man's parents through a carefully chosen and respectable mediator. In the same spirit one cannot approach a chief or king directly, but must have one's case brought through a sub-chief. It is therefore conceivable that God, by virtue of being parent of all — the greatest and most powerful being, Creator and thus Great Ancestor of all — must be approached through intermediaries. The ancestor spirits, close to both the living and the Supreme Being, are most qualified to function as intermediaries. Therefore, the Christian idea of a mediator between God and humanity was no new concept to Zimbabwean traditional beliefs. What they could not understand was the concept of a single mediator for all of humanity.

Traditionalists see the ancestors as guardian spirits and intermediaries, responsible to God for all their actions. Even if God's name is not always mentioned during prayers and sacrifices, it is believed that God is their ultimate recipient. But like the living elders, ancestors can get angry and demand that they be appeased. In some traditions, therefore, it becomes difficult to distinguish whether prayers or sacrifices are being addressed to God or to the ancestor. Some Shona traditionalists, when asked whether they worship ancestors, will say that as far as they are concerned God and the ancestors are one and the same, and an address to one is an address to the other. In this sense one might speak of "ancestor-worship", but such worship is clearly secondary, intended to facilitate worship of the Supreme Being. Sacrifices are made to them in the understanding that they enjoy a special relationship with the Supreme Being, so that even if at times one does not hear the name of God mentioned, it does not mean that the people do not worship God. For example, children are seen as a gift of *Mwari* (God) and the *vadzimu* (ancestors). One often hears the expression "*Kana Mwari nevadzimu vachida*" (if God and the ancestors are willing). People faced with misfortune will say, "*Ko Mwari wati ndaita sei?*" (What crime does God accuse me of?) or "*Mudzimu yafuratira*" (The ancestors have turned their backs on us).

In traditional societies, death is not the end but a change of status and form of being. The dead continue to play important roles as intermediaries and guardians of their descendants. They can therefore be addressed in the event of a family misfortune, beginning with the recently deceased father. It is generally presumed, although not always explicitly stated, that the oldest member of the family reports to the Supreme Being who is ultimately the recipient of all worship or praise. One must always be careful not to offend the ancestor spirits. They may punish severely. Although they are believed rarely to cause the death of their descendants, they can make life very uncomfortable by bringing about sickness, misfortune, misbehaviour in children, mental derangement and the like.

It is believed that the "living dead" want to participate in every activity of the family. When you eat it is necessary to share the food with them, when you go on a journey they must be informed, in a marriage they must receive their share of the bride's wealth. If they are not consulted or given their share, they will get angry and cause some misfortune. Members of the family who do not participate in the family rituals bring misfortune not only on themselves but also on the other family members. This creates a pressure to participate which obviously causes many problems for those who have become Christian while other family members remain traditionalists.

What then does all this mean for the gospel and culture encounter in Zimbabwe? If the people already knew God through "natural revelation" (Rom. 1:18ff.), and if they already worshipped God — however imperfectly — through the departed elders, perhaps all they needed to hear was that God has affirmed his commitment to them through the incarnation, death and resurrection of his Son. I believe this was the message of the first heralds of the gospel to the people of Zimbabwe. The question is what this message meant in the context of a culture that is religious as well as in the context of the people's struggle for liberation from colonialism. How did that message find its way into such a culture and how was it perceived? In the light of Zimbabwean cultures and religious traditions, how did the missionaries relate the gospel?

NOTES

[1] H. Richard Niebuhr, *Christ and Culture*, New York, Harper & Row, 1956, p.32.
[2] See A. Moyo, "The Quest for African Theology and the Problem of the Relationship Between Faith and Culture: The Hermeneutical Perspective", *African Theological Journal*, Vol. 12, 1983, pp.95-108.
[3] Immanuel K. Twesigye, *Common Ground: Christianity, African Religion and Philosophy*, New York, Peter Lang, 1987, p.93.
[4] *Ibid*. p.94.

2. Gospel, Culture and Christian Missions

The first encounter between gospel and culture in Zimbabwe came in 1560, when the Catholic bishop of Mozambique sent a group of Jesuit missionaries, led by Father Gonzalo da Silveira. During a brief stop in a Tonga town whose chief had asked the bishop for missionaries,[1] Silveira claimed to have baptized 450 persons, but his report to the authorities in Goa makes it clear that he and his team never seriously engaged the Tonga people and their culture in a dialogue with the gospel. The Christian community they founded appears to have lasted only as long as they were there. Silveira reported:

> I made a point of baptizing a large number together immediately, because these people resemble children who like to act together and follow each other's lead. They also resemble children as far as their intellectual impediment in receiving the faith is concerned, for none of them have any kind of idol or form of worship resembling idolatry.[2]

This statement shows that Silveira made the mistake of equating the African communal way of living with childlike behaviour. Since religion for the Tonga people was not an affair for the individual, their response to the preaching of the gospel could only be communal. The issues raised by the gospel were of so serious a nature that no member of the community should be left out. If they understood the gospel as offering new life to the community, they could not allow that kind of life to be the property of individuals in their community. Life through faith in Christ was freely given by God himself to be shared by all in the community and to be passed on to all members of the community, past and present. So in terms of the Tonga traditional thought, the response to the gospel could only be communal. Because Silveira expected an individual response, which was contrary to the Tonga way of looking at things, he concluded that they were like children. The available sources do not make it clear what had attracted the Tonga chief to invite the Portuguese to send missionaries, but from the look of things it could not have been the missionaries' religion.

Silveira's other error was to believe that the Tonga people had no meaningful religious experience prior to their encounter with the gospel message. He failed to realize that religion for the Tonga was a way of life, and that the absence of idols and temples and worship services and the other religious symbols he was familiar with was no sign that the Tonga did not have religious beliefs of their own. His encounter with these people was superficial; hence, the gospel that he preached also remained superficial, neither challenging nor entering into dialogue with Tonga culture and religion. His new converts seem not to have understood what Christianity was all about, nor what they were committing themselves to when they submitted themselves for baptism.

When Silveira finally arrived in Zimbabwe, the capital of Mwenemotapa's empire, his approach and style of ministry were the same. Silveira's very first encounter with the emperor produced misunderstanding, again as a result of different cultural perspectives and expectations. Upon his arrival, Silveira was received by the emperor as an honoured guest, and was offered gold, cattle and the choice of any of the king's daughters as a wife. This gesture of hospitality Silveira and his party declined, saying they preferred spiritual pursuits to material things.[3] The result was that Silveira was grossly misunderstood. The gifts were a way of saying to these messengers of the gospel, "You are welcome! Feel at home!" The emperor is said to have felt very much insulted by the behaviour of the mission party and to have wondered whether a man who refused such gifts was indeed human. Here was a real encounter between two cultures, and the gospel was caught in the crossfire.

However, the report goes on to say that the emperor soon submitted to baptism, together with hundreds of his people. Again, the question is whether these conversions were real. Not long thereafter, the emperor turned against his guests and executed Silveira. The missionary became the victim of a very dynamic encounter between two cultures, two religious traditions and two competing worldviews.

These 16th-century missions ended in dismal failure, whereas the renewed efforts towards the end of the 19th century finally yielded some positive results. D.N. Beach has demonstrated that these later Christian missions among the Shona peoples often began with the arrival of an African evangelist to preach the gospel, laying the groundwork for the establishment of a mission station with the subsequent arrival and settlement of a white missionary,[4] who was also often accompanied by African evangelists. Beach concludes that "a great deal of work was carried out by devoted and determined African evangelists, and in many ways the establishment of Christianity was as much an African achievement as a European one."[5]

With zeal all these missionaries preached Christ crucified, risen from the dead and alive today. But the Christ they proclaimed was *above* African culture and *against* African culture, clearly not *in* African culture. Both white and black missionaries understood conversion to Christianity as meaning the adoption of a European style of living. Relations with the departed ancestors were declared idolatry, any Christian marriage had to be monogamous, and initiation practices must be given up. African culture had to be destroyed and replaced with something very different, and that new thing was in fact identical with Western culture. What was needed, however, was a Christ who would renew or transform African culture. While the African peoples had many ideas about life which God had revealed to them, there was also a great deal of imperfection in their cultures. The need was to allow the gospel to enter these cultures in order to adopt and adapt, renew and purify them from within and present them to God as living sacrifice. The proclamation of the gospel ought to have allowed the people and their cultures to come alive, not to make them feel rejected.

The extension of colonial power to the whole of southern and central Africa had an evident impact on the activities of Christian missions and the establishment of the church in the region. With the conquest of the Africans the heralds of the gospel could now carry out their mission under the protection and with the help of the colonial powers. The European missionaries, aided by the African evangelists, could now begin to build churches in a manner not permitted by the African political leaders. Albert Plangger has noted that the first Jesuit missionaries to Zimbabwe in the 19th-century "were tolerated but not really permitted to establish themselves as church workers".[6] The setting up of colonial administrations dramatically changed that. The European colonial powers saw the missionaries as partners in a campaign to civilize the "natives". The colonizer gave land to mission organizations, and this land continues to be owned by those churches.[7] On these lands churches built schools and hospitals and created mission reserves for their converts. These became platforms from which to reach the Africans with the gospel. Christian missions met with considerable success, and the Christian church soon became firmly established throughout most of Africa south of the Sahara.

The success of the Christian missions in Zimbabwe was due not only to the white missionaries but also to the new converts, particularly the poor evangelists, who embraced the faith enthusiastically and actively preached the gospel to their own people. The following extract from a report made in 1911 to the American Methodist Umtali District Conference is illuminating:

> In nearly every case [converts] have been brought to Christ through the influence of Christian natives. Many times the Christian community, with its higher and better standard of living, seems to have appealed to [them]. These Christian men and women command the utmost respect of the heathen people. It is giving them an example of a ripe fruit of Christianity at this stage of their development. I believe that a group of such Christian laymen, who live the normal Christian life, who of course preach also, but depend upon manual labour for their living, make a mighty strong evangelizing agent... The boys I have talked to very frequently mention some native preacher who seemed to have helped them very much. The boys have very seldom said they were helped by white missionaries. I

> suppose these spiritual matters require close heart-to-heart talks that are more likely to occur between two natives than between a native and a white man. Further it is not possible for the few white men that we have to reach any number of people personally. But there is also a considerable number who profess Christianity in the isolated *kraals* through the preaching of boys who have been to mines or to schools.[8]

Despite this acknowledgment that the gospel is more effectively communicated by people who share the same cultural perspectives, the European missionary's perspective on gospel and culture still dominated, and the Christianity that was established remained basically Western in its cultural outlook. However, it is well known that the African Christians in actual fact retained within their Christian faith and practice many of the aspects of the traditional cultures — particularly those pertaining to relations with the living dead, recognition of the role of diviners and belief in the power of witchcraft — which the mission churches condemned as contrary to the gospel message and the Christian way of life.

The translation of the Bible into the African languages shows that sooner or later the missionaries recognized the need to build on African cultures and to communicate with the African people through the local symbols. There is no doubt that a people's language is the most important bearer of its culture. The translators may not have been aware that by translating the gospel into African languages they were actually engaged in enculturating the gospel in Africa and thus in dialogue with African culture and religion, but by identifying the Supreme Being of African religions, Mwari or uNkulunkulu, with God the Father of Jesus Christ revealed in the Bible, Christian missionaries to Zimbabwe were indeed affirming the unity and the universality of the Godhead, and in that way also the African traditional idea of God, known to them through general revelation (Rom. 1:18ff.).

Even so, the traditional Christian approach to mission continued for the most part to deny any knowledge of the true

God in African traditional cultures. Alongside the affirmation of the richness of the traditional beliefs about God, the majority of missionaries still insisted that African traditional religions were mere superstition.

Those who converted to Christianity were expected to adopt the white man's culture which came with it. In some cases converts were moved into "mission reserves", not only to protect them from harassment by their people, but also to enable them to adopt a new style of living and a new, European culture. Under the label of fighting "ignorance" and "superstition", mission schools and hospitals were also intended to create a new African who would reject his or her culture and its traditional methods of healing and education in favour of Western ones. Exposed on the "mission reserves" and through the new educational system to Western foods, music, dance, education and medicine — in short, a Western life-style — many African Christians began to despise their own cultures.

This short summary of aspects of missionary history in Zimbabwe shows that it is not possible to communicate the gospel without a good understanding of African traditional cultures and religions. The encounter was equally between the missionary and the Zimbabwean, and between the gospel and the indigenous cultures of Zimbabwe. Most early missionaries were apparently far more enthusiastic about preaching the gospel than about learning the cultures of the peoples whom they encountered. In some cases the results were fatal, leaving a trail of martyrs.

The question this raises is whether there is an alternative approach in which the missionaries could have communicated only the gospel, rather than insisting that those who became Christians should adopt the missionaries' style of living. The gospel and culture issue is about human beings who are called to faith in God through Christ and to live out that faith. How have the Zimbabweans, after a little more than a century of Christian influence, been able to live out that faith within the context of their traditional cultures and the Western cultures which mediated the gospel message? Is there a Zimbabwean Christian culture which has emerged? If so, how far is it a transformation of the traditional cultures? Has anything changed at all, or is it the traditional way of living to which faith in Christ has been added in a syncretistic manner?

NOTES

[1] Cf. J.M. Chirenge, "Portuguese Priests and Soldiers in Zimbabwe 1560-1572. The Interplay Between Evangelism and Trade", *International Journal of African Historical Studies*, Vol. 4, 1974, pp.39f. For other useful studies of the history of Christian missions in Zimbabwe see H. Bhila, "Trade and Early Missionaries in Southern Zambezia" and other articles in M.F.C. Bourdillon, ed., *Christianity South of the Zambezi*, Vol. 2, Gweru, Mambo Press, 1977, pp.25-42; and J.A. Dachs, ed., *Christianity South of the Zambezi*, Vol. 1, Gweru, Mambo Press, 1973.

[2] Cited from Chirenge, *op. cit.*, p.40.

[3] Cf. the discussion in J. du Plessis, *A History of Christian Missions in Africa*, Cape Town, E. Struck, 1911; Bhila, *op. cit.*, p.25, refers to information in other sources which say that Silveira passed the cattle to his friend Caido.

[4] D.N. Beach, "The Initial Impact of Christianity on the Shona: The Protestants and the Southern Shona", in Dachs, *op. cit.*, pp.25-40.

[5] *Ibid.*, p.27.

[6] Albert B. Plangger, "Human Rights: A Motive for Mission", in C.F. Hallencreutz and A. Moyo, eds, *Church and State in Zimbabwe*, Gweru, Mambo Press, 1988, p.443.

[7] On the land issue in Zimbabwe, see the study of Sebastian Bakare, Zimbabwe, 1994.

[8] Cited by T.O. Ranger, "Religion, Development and African Christian Identity", in Kirsten H. Peterson, ed., *Religion, Development and African Identity*, Uppsala, Scandinavian Institute of African Studies, 1987, p.37.

3. Gospel, Culture and Christian Life

The church in Zimbabwe, as in most countries in southern Africa, is very much alive and growing rapidly. Most African churches today are self-governing, self-propagating and in many respects also self-supporting.

We have seen that the traditional Christian approach to mission involved a complete rejection of traditional cultures and religious beliefs and practices. In the mainline churches today, this official attitude remains despite the change in leadership from foreign missionaries to African Christians. The result for many African Christians is that endeavouring to be genuine disciples of Christ in the image presented to them in the teaching of the church is a source of conflict. Many have been able to dissociate themselves from their traditional religious beliefs and so have nothing to do with their ancestors or the beliefs associated with witchcraft and divination, often leaving them rather isolated from their people. Many other Christians have on their own comfortably integrated their Christian faith into the traditional cultures and participate in rituals relating to the ancestors without any feeling of guilt.

In this chapter we shall examine the impact of African cultures on the lives of Zimbabwean Christians, in order to see how, in the light of the mainline Christian approach to mission and Christian living, many of them have insisted on retaining a part of their traditional cultures and beliefs, including the relations with ancestors, and what this means for their understanding of the gospel. In the African way of living, as we have seen, life can be meaningful only if it is life in communion with and among your people. This way of life is based on a kinship system that any discussion of gospel and culture in Zimbabwe must take into account, as it reflects a very important aspect of the African worldview.

Despite the official teaching of the church, the faith and practice of many Zimbabwean Christians might lead an outside observer to conclude that Christianity in Zimbabwe is a synthesis of faith in Jesus Christ with traditional religious beliefs and practices. This applies to persons in both urban and rural settings, although this distinction is not exclusive, since most so-called urban or highly educated Zimbabweans live in both societies. Those who own beautiful houses in a city like Harare, possibly even with several acres of land attached, might feel that place to be their permanent home. However, according to African tradition, such a home cannot be permanent but only a place of residence for the purpose of employment in Harare. The real home is out in the communal lands where one's people live. It is there that one is entitled to a piece of land to build one's own home, and indeed many of those living and working in towns do so. It is there that they are expected to be buried when they die — and this may be done even against their own will or that of their spouse. It is there that they are expected to spend their holidays or celebrate the most important festivals of the year. Home is "where you go for Christmas or for Easter", where your people live, and these include both the living and the living dead. Since the African community is made up of the living and the living dead, the land belongs equally to both, and the living dead are in fact believed to be its guardians. Hence, people continue to interact with them and to share everything they have with them.

Such strong family or communal ties demand participation in the life of the extended family. This means that urbanized Zimbabweans who still feel a sense of kinship to their people in the communal lands cannot help participating in one way or other in the life of the rural community, with its holistic approach to life, in which religion is inseparable from culture. The extended family concept forces one into the community. Where a family is made up of both Christians and African traditionalists, many Christians find themselves taking part in one way or another in the traditional ceremonies. For some the religious aspects which are inseparable from these ceremonies are a source of conflict and difficult to handle.

To understand this, one must bear in mind the strong belief in African traditional religions that death is not the end of life. At one level this presents no problems for Christians since this belief is confirmed in the gospel message. The difficulty arises from the further belief that those who die become the "living dead" (*mudzimu/idhlozi*). To become a *mudzimu/idhlozi*, one must be brought back home in a special ceremony, and if this is not done it can only result in a great deal of sickness and misfortune being inflicted on the family by the spirit of the deceased person. Many African Christians, including highly educated ones, believe this, and so some of them not only participate in but even organize such ceremonies for their deceased parents. When sickness or misfortune strikes a family, many begin to wonder whether it was not caused by one of their ancestors, particularly if the bringing home ceremony has not been done. Because of the extended family system, the person may be advised or even required to join a family delegation to consult a traditional diviner to find out the cause of the misfortune. Today many traditional diviners operate in urban areas and even rent offices right in the centre of the cities.

The point is that many Zimbabweans today can be called Christian traditionalists, happily living in accordance with their traditional culture, while very much convinced of and devoted to the message of the gospel. The gospel has become a part of their culture, but the ancestors cannot be wished away from their communities and they see no conflict in the way they relate to them and to the gospel. Traditional methods of healing and divination do not pose a challenge to a person who believes in both the general and the special revelation of God.

The traditional Christian mission approach to African traditional culture evidently left the gospel *above* African culture. The phenomenon described here shows that many individual Christians have taken the initiative to find a place for the gospel *in* their culture. Many could not conceive a life without the "living dead" members of their family. What difference is there between praying to the ancestors and to the saints? The African peoples knew very well in their traditional religious beliefs that the "living dead" derive their power from God and as intermediaries do not function independently of God. When the church condemned traditional rites of passage and rituals related to departed members of the family, many Christians felt a vacuum which they could not ignore if their spiritual needs were to be fully satisfied. By rejecting the possibility of relations with the "living dead", Christian preaching in Zimbabwe failed to recognize that its message was not complete as far as its listeners were concerned, for it excluded part of the family. While many Christians today manifest respect for departed ancestors and take part in ceremonies relating to them openly, many others do so only privately. They live a Christian life during the day, and live the real African life during the night, resulting in what Desmond Tutu and others have described as a kind of schizophrenia:

> Until fairly recently, the African Christian has suffered from a form of schizophrenia. With part of himself he has been compelled to pay lip service to Christianity as understood, expressed and preached by the white man. But with an ever greater part of himself, a part he has often been ashamed to acknowledge openly and which he has struggled to repress, he has felt that his Africanness was being violated. The white man's largely cerebral religion hardly touched the depths of his African soul; he was being redeemed from sins he did not believe he had committed; he was being given answers, and often splendid answers, to questions he had not asked.[1]

It is common among Zimbabwean Christians of all denominations, including pastors, to participate, in times of prolonged illness or other misfortune in the family, in the traditional rituals relating to the departed elders. Some Christians stop going to church or stay away from the Lord's supper or active participation in church life for a while in order to give themselves time to perform the traditional rites and make the required sacrifices to bring about healing in the family. When they have completed what the traditional diviners have prescribed in relation to the departed elders and spirits, they return to the church authorities to request absolution. African pastors who are close to their people know that these things are happening in both the rural and urban settings.

What this shows is that African cultures today, though very influenced by the Western style of living, have retained many of their own characteristics. The African worldview continues to be very much alive for the majority of Zimbabweans. The challenge for the African church is to be able to affirm both the uniqueness of Christ and his supremacy within African cultures. This means taking the African experience and cultures seriously and allowing them also to participate in the transforming power of the gospel, so that in them and through them the love of Christ might be made manifest. In the different cultures God has laid a foundation. As Hatendi has observed, "the commission to 'Go and make disciples of all nations' does not authorize the missionary to ignore or destroy the foundation which God himself has laid, for the grace of God takes nature (natural revelation) for granted."[2]

To understand how the Christian traditionalist perceives the gospel, one must bear in mind that the African worldview sees all of what happens or is in this world from an holistic perspective. The spiritual and the physical worlds overlap and cannot be separated. The African's ontology is through and through religious. Discussions with those whom I have called Christian traditionalists in Zimbabwe show how they have been able to integrate their Christian faith into their traditional cultures without feeling any conflict, seeing this rather as a natural development or manner in which the gospel finds its way into a people's culture and becomes alive in that culture. Culture provides new symbols for understanding or articulating theological perceptions.

If Christianity is a force to be reckoned with in Zimbabwe today, and if culture is all-inclusive, what impact has the gospel made on the development of the national life of Zimbabwe since independence? Does the gospel have a contribution to make to the process of nation-building and liberation in independent Zimbabwe?

NOTES

[1] Desmond M. Tutu, "Whither African Theology?", in Edward Fashole-Luke, Richard Grey, Adrian Hastings and Godwin Tasie, eds, *Christianity in Independent Africa*, London, Rex Collins, 1978, p.366.
[2] R.P. Hatendi, "Shona Marriage and the Christian Churches", in Dachs, *Christianity South of the Zambezi*, p.147.

4. Gospel and Culture and the State

When Zimbabwe became independent in 1980, its leaders openly declared their desire to be guided by Marxist-Leninist principles in their search for a different social and economic system for the country. That ideology was reinterpreted to ensure that it did not ignore the realities of the particular situation prevailing in Zimbabwe:

> In our approach to socio-economic phenomena, we insist that Zimbabwean life itself, the hard facts of reality, our objective circumstances, should be taken into account when applying the principles of Marxism and Leninism. While we value other countries' experiences, we are opposed to importing a carbon-copy socialist system with outworn formulas, presuppositions and dogmas that are foreign to our geo-political and historical situation. We are not doctrinaire or dogmatic.[1]

They believed they could use the instruments derived from scientific socialism to bring about the social, economic and political changes needed to benefit the majority of the people of Zimbabwe. However, contrary to classical Marxism and Leninism, which saw religion as "the opium of the people", they saw Christianity with its message as a natural ally in bringing about the cultural transformation of Zimbabwean society:

> Whatever strategy of socialist transformation the state adopts, the need to harness allies will continue forcefully to present itself. Thus, if the morality of socialism is also the morality of Christian teaching in respect of humanistic values it cherishes, the state and the church must see themselves as allies rather than as vying opponents.[2]

Indeed, the government believed that its vision of the new society in Zimbabwe was identical with the Christian vision of society:

> The Christian vision of society is an extension of the Christian vision of man, the core of which is the primacy of the person, that is, the value and worth which the human person derives from being created in the image of God. If the primacy of the human person is to be validated in history, then the concern to

incarnate the Christian vision of society should be a concern for development.[3]

It was the strong view of Prime Minister Robert Mugabe and, indeed, many other Zimbabweans that, in the light of their experiences over the years, the capitalist ethos was contrary both to the spirit of the gospel of Christ and to the African way of thinking:

> The elimination of an individualistic society, with its attributes of inequality and selfishness, and its replacement by a collectivistic society, is undoubtedly a moral philosophy. When we talk of socialism versus capitalism we are actually talking of morality versus immorality, equity versus inequity, humanity versus inhumanity, and, I dare say, Christianity versus unchristianity.[4]

In an address to church leaders in Zimbabwe, Mugabe stated quite clearly: "In my view, Christians should feel more at home in a socialist environment than in a capitalist one."[5]

At that time Zimbabwe had just emerged from a very oppressive and dehumanizing social, economic and political system which, however, claimed to be an ally of Christianity. Having rejected that alliance, the Zimbabweans began to look for a system that would incarnate the values of the Christian message in the culture or society of the people of Zimbabwe. Whereas the church sought to transform the human person in Zimbabwe through the preaching of the gospel of Christ, the state believed it could use the instruments derived from Marxism and Leninism to work together with the church to bring about that new society. It sought to harness all progressive forces for the good of all Zimbabweans, and one such force was the call of the church to live out the message of the gospel in society.

When Zimbabwe became independent, there were fears that a black majority government under Marxist-Leninist inspired leadership, which eventually won the first general elections, would move swiftly against all religious practices and observances. However, already in their election manifestos those very leaders had not only promised that they would guarantee religious freedom to all Zimbabweans but also committed themselves to promoting the work of the church. Despite the distortions of the gospel from which they had suffered in their relations with white Rhodesian Christians like Ian Smith — and, indeed, from many white missionaries, some of whom accepted conscription into the Rhodesian army to fight against the people to whom they had been sent by their home boards with the gospel message — Zimbabweans saw the church, with its message of love, forgiveness and reconciliation through faith in Jesus Christ, as a natural ally in nation-building. They had chosen reconciliation as the cornerstone of their policies.

Even more telling for an understanding of the relationship between gospel and culture in Zimbabwe is the way that the new government moved immediately after independence to convert what might have been seen as campaign rhetoric into reality. Barely two years into independence, the so-called Marxist-Leninist government issued a directive requiring the teaching of religious education in primary and secondary schools in Zimbabwe. To this day, this is basically Christian education, despite the official government policy that it should be multi-faith in its approach and content in order to expose students to a variety of religious traditions. The use of the book series *Developing in Christ* by the government ministry of education clearly shows that the bias is in favour of Christianity. Pupils are required to learn the subject together, as is the case in any other subject, under the same religious instructor. From the government perspective the teachers are prohibited from indoctrinating or evangelizing the pupils.

To understand these developments, one must bear in mind the religious background of the people of Zimbabwe. The nation was born out of a bitter armed conflict in which the peasants, both Christian and non-Christian, played a key role. In the rural areas the guerrillas had worked very closely with both the spirit mediums and the local church leadership. Memories of spirit mediums such as Mbuya Nehanda and Sekuru Kaguvi, both of whom were executed in the first war of liberation (Chimurenga) in 1890, provided a great deal of inspiration to the struggling masses and to the freedom fighters. Ranger sums up the role of traditional religions, and in particular the spirit mediums, in Zimbabwe's struggle for liberation:

> It is they who offered the most effective means of bringing together peasant elders, who had hitherto been the local leaders of radical opposition, with the young strangers who entered each district, armed with guns and ready to administer revolutionary law. Hence not only peasants but most guerrillas came to draw most heavily on the religious elements within the composite ideology of the war.[6]

Their experiences growing up in traditional societies and their continued relation to those societies made it clear to the leadership that religion is an integral part of their people's lives and that any attack on their religions would be understood as an attack on the people themselves. Religion can neither be separated from all other aspects of human existence nor reduced to a private, individual affair. Religion is part and parcel of life, permeating everything, and cannot be compartmentalized. It provides the moral fibre which needs to be maintained. The secular authorities thus had no option but to recognize the religious basis of African culture. The spirit mediums, who are the prophetic leaders of African societies, served as one point of reference through which African culture and religion could be incorporated into the ideology of Marxism-Leninism. However, it was also clear that the local and the universal Christian communities had a message which had inspired many Zimbabweans to reject the inhumanity of a system denying fellow human beings the freedom that comes with being created in the image of God and, therefore, to reject the alleged close alliance between gospel and Western culture. This meant that the gospel, which had also become a dominant aspect of Zimbabwean culture, could also be accommodated within that composite state ideology whose goal was to create a new society.

NOTES

[1] Deputy Prime Minister Simon Muzenda, cited in Hallencreutz and Moyo, eds, *Church and State in Zimbabwe*, p.210.
[2] Prime Minister Robert G. Mugabe, cited in *ibid.*, p.210.
[3] Canaan Banana (first president of Zimbabwe), cited in *ibid.*, p.211.
[4] Mugabe, cited in *ibid.*, p.211.
[5] *Ibid.*
[6] Ranger, *Peasant Consciousness and Guerrilla Warfare in Zimbabwe*, London, James Currey, 1985, p.189.

5. Gospel and Culture in the African Independent Churches

We have seen that despite the mission churches' rejection of their traditional culture, many African Christians in these churches have been able to integrate much of traditional beliefs, customs and practices into their way of life. There is, however, another side of Christianity in Zimbabwe (as elsewhere in Africa), which casts a great deal of light on the question of the relationship between gospel and culture. This is the rise of African Independent Churches, often as an expression of resistance to the idea that accepting the gospel means completely rejecting traditional cultures.[1]

The first of these independent churches appeared in western and southern Africa. Historically, most of the African Independent Churches in Zimbabwe originated in South Africa, from where they were brought to Zimbabwe by migrant workers, but they soon acquired a distinct character of their own, multiplying rapidly particularly among the Southern Shona people.

The beginnings of these movements can be traced back to a Congolese woman named Donna Beatrice, who as early as 1700 claimed to have been possessed by the spirit of St Anthony. Her message was that Christ and the apostles were blacks who lived in Sao Salvador (the present Angola). This was the first recorded cry from black Africa for an indigenous Christ, expressing a deep "yearning for a Christ who would identify with the despised African" and raising the basic question, "How could the white Christ of the Portuguese images, the Christ of the exploiters..., ever help the suffering African, pining for liberty?"[2] How could the African people claim for themselves this same Christ who has remained above their culture? As Taylor says, the rise of the African Independent Churches was no doubt a reaction against a Christ who was presented to them "as the answer to questions a white man would ask, the solution to the needs that Western man would feel, the Saviour of the European worldview, the object of adoration and prayer of historic Christendom".[3] They sought a Christ who would be known by the African people as a brother, one who would answer the questions they were asking and redeem humanity as they themselves understood and experienced it.

Today African Independent Churches are a visible and formidable force throughout most of Zimbabwe. Some began as revival movements within the mainline churches and had no intention of breaking away. The crucial factor was the desire of African Christians to feel at home in church, to give voice to their Christianity in African symbols and images. Christianity as proclaimed by the missionaries was not comprehensive enough to meet their spiritual needs, and the historical churches made no serious attempt to understand African traditional spirituality and culture as whole.

Moreover, as far as the African people were concerned, missionaries and the colonial settlers were birds of a feather, and each was blamed for the immorality of the other. After all, they did share a common worldview, which they all claimed to be Christian, and a common perception of the African. David Livingstone, the famous missionary and explorer who was the first white person to see the Victoria Falls, wrote:

> We come among them as members of a superior race and servants of a government that desires to elevate the more degraded portions of the human family. We are adherents of a benign, holy religion and merely by consistent conduct and wise, patient efforts become harbingers of peace to a hitherto distracted and downtrodden race.[4]

It was common in Zimbabwe for many missionaries not only to tolerate but even to practise discrimination, to the extent of providing racially separate sections in sanctuaries. Many independent church members cite such racism as the reason for their leaving the mainline churches. One member of the Zionist church put it this way:

> The Dutch Reformed Church does not honour an African as a human being... The missionaries even close their doors on us when they have their meals. We Zionists differ in this respect, because we recognize each other as true Africans, real people created by God. Therefore we are a wonderful church.[5]

Another independent church member said:

> I joined the Topia Church because the Dutch Reformed Church were not interested in my fate. Four of my children died. On one occasion I informed the church leaders at the mission what had happened, but they refused to come to the burial of my child. I told my uncle Chipinga, who arrived with some Topia members at my homestead, to assist me. They conducted the burial ceremony, provided the cloth to wrap up the corpse and they consoled me. On another occasion the DRC officials promised to come and conduct the burial of another child. But they never arrived. Again vaTopia assisted me. This time I was convinced and I joined their ranks.[6]

The missionary practice to "distinguish the colour of the skin" (*kushara ganda*) was indeed widespread. According to one independent church leader, "The American Board missionaries failed to realize that we have come of age. They fail to realize real love to the Africans. We are not allowed to enter the same places as they." By practising segregation in its institutions and sanctuaries, the church unwittingly "preached against itself and violated human rights".[7]

But in addition to these contradictions between what people heard missionaries preach and saw them practise, another factor which contributed significantly to the establishment of some African Independent Churches was the translation of the Bible into African languages. Once African Christians could read and interpret the Bible for themselves they discovered that such paradigms of biblical faith as Abraham and David were polygamists. The mainline churches recognized only monogamous marriages, preferably solemnized by a certified government marriage officer, who might be a priest or a magistrate. Marriage in this respect is clearly seen as a secular institution to which the church lends its blessing for those who are Christians. But many Zimbabwean Christians still prefer to have their marriages solemnized according to African customary law because, as Hatendi observes, "they understand customary marriage better than the Western". Many Zimbabweans do not see any sense

> in marrying as the whites marry in the suburbs of Salisbury (Harare) and not as they marry in the Shona tribal lands, a community where a couple will spend most of their time together... It is also doubtful that Africans are convinced by the teaching of the missionaries on marriage, for they do not feel it a sin to marry according to African custom. What is important for them is to *be seen and accepted as married persons by their family groups and community,* for marriage is essentially of the community.[8]

In the eyes of the members of the independent churches the gospel is not against customary marriage law, and monogamy and the solemnization of marriages by government officers are a cultural imposition on the African people which have nothing to do with the salvation of the individual.

Furthermore, the independent church members discovered through reading the Bible that the ten commandments demand that parents be honoured. Indeed, this is the only commandment that comes with a promise, namely, "so that your days may be long in the land" (Ex. 20:12). For the African peoples the "parents" include the ancestors or the "living dead". They can identify themselves with Abraham, Isaac and Jacob as far as their way of life is concerned. Moreover, when Jesus, discussing the resurrection, reminded his followers that God had said in the scriptures, "I am the God of Abraham, Isaac, and Jacob", he went on to explain that this means that God is God, "not of the dead, but of the living" (Matt. 22:31f.). Can this not be understood by someone from an African traditional religious background as an affirmation that Abraham, Isaac and Jacob are alive as the "living dead" in traditional religious belief?

The marriage customs and family life of the patriarchs also have a great deal in common with those of many African cultures. Jesus' remarks about the resurrection cited above were made in a discussion that began when the Sadducees quoted a saying of Moses that "if a man dies childless, his brother shall marry the widow, and raise up children for his brother" (Matt. 22:24). This is common practice in many African cultures in Zimbabwe. Jesus raises no objection to this practice, but simply focusses on the resurrection.

Thus the translation of the Bible into African languages was the beginning of the translation of the gospel into African culture; and the significant contribution this made to the development of indigenous African Christian spirituality is evident in the African Independent Churches.

Other factors which helped to create a climate in which Africans began to search for the kind of spirituality that would relate to their own political ambitions and maintain an ethos in line with their own traditional culture and spirituality include the reluctance or even refusal of missionaries to relinquish church leadership to the indigenous people, their discouragement of faith healing, prophesy and speaking in tongues — all of which were practised in the early church — and their negative attitudes towards polygamy, ancestor veneration, witches and traditional medicine.

The African Independent Churches represent a serious attempt to bring the gospel into the African culture by expressing it in images familiar to the African people and in responding concretely to their needs and aspirations. These movements take the African worldview seriously by making it clear in their faith and practice that in an African cultural context salvation must include the offer of protection against magic, sorcery and witchcraft. It is noteworthy that most African Independent Churches uncompromisingly oppose participation in the traditional rites related to veneration of the ancestors or divination through the traditional diviner. However, the role of prophecy becomes very significant in bridging the gap between the gospel and their African culture. Some prophets behave very much like the spirit mediums in Shona traditional religions. Bourdillon describes the case of a prophet possessed by the Holy Spirit, speaking

> in a lilting voice typical of lion spirit mediums and uttering groans, sighs and other sounds associated with lion spirits..., [they] may twitch and shake as possessed mediums do...., may [at the beginning of prophecy] utter an incomprehensible jumble of names and phrases from the Bible, just as a medium at the beginning of a seance may utter a jumble of names from the traditional history of the chiefdom to which he belongs.[9]

Many parallels could also be pointed out between the activities of the prophet and the traditional diviner. In a way, it could be said that the prophet takes over the place and the functions of the traditional diviner and spirit medium. Possessed by the Holy Spirit, rather than the spirit of an ancestor, he or she is responsible for detecting the witches or the causes of illness and death, and determining what needs to be done to protect the individual and family. Thus it is the prophet who now goes to the homestead of the person haunted by witches or evil powers to remove whatever the witches may have buried there to cause sickness and death, and who takes concrete steps through prayer, holy water or special ropes to protect its members from the negative forces. The use of ropes appears to take the place of the protective amulets worn by traditionalists to protect themselves against witches and sorcerers. These ropes thus symbolize Christ's power and victory over the evil spirits. The prophet also organizes and officiates at rain-making ceremonies, taking the place of the traditional rain mediums. The prophet's ability to heal the sick replaces another one of the functions of the traditional diviners.

While the independent churches are able in these ways to fill the vacuum created by their rejection of traditional rites, there are also some significant differences between prophets and spirit mediums. Prophetic divination can only be through the Holy Spirit and never through communication with the ancestors. It is the Holy Spirit that helps the prophet to detect witches, adulterers and other persons in the community who behave in anti-social ways and to explain the causes of misfortune (which explanations are often the same as those in traditional thought). In independent churches of the Spirit type, speaking in tongues is a gift to all members, but unlike in traditional ceremonies, where there will be many people at the same time possessed by different spirits, the Christians in these movements will all be possessed by the Holy Spirit, and, when possessed, both the prophets and members speak in their natural voices.

It is clear that the mainline churches have been unable, in their official or confessional stances, to take the gospel into African culture. The gospel has been very much *above* traditional cultures, though as we have said earlier there has been a great deal of "unofficial" integration of gospel with traditional culture even in mainline Christianity. Bourdillon rightly concludes that

> the popular independent churches have managed to combine traditional ways of thinking and acting with the new international religion based on a high God who cares for all people and who can be approached by anyone. They are thus able to cope with the transition from traditional tribal communities to contact with the wider international world.[10]

African Independent Churches recognize that since religion permeates the entire traditional African way of life and cannot be isolated, Christianity must bring Christ into all of African culture if it is to succeed. The prophetic leader in the independent church is seen as an *African* religious leader, who is not to be confused with the diviner but nevertheless gains respect by meeting those needs which were met by the diviner. Since African people were already religious before the preaching of the gospel to them, since they already knew God, there was a point of contact at which the dialogue between the gospel and African cultures could begin, a common experience based on knowledge of God as the Creator and Sustainer of the universe.

The gospel is about the revelation of that same God in Jesus Christ through culture and in culture. It is about God becoming human, becoming visible in culture, remaining in culture and yet remaining above culture. It is about God seeking a new relationship with the whole creation, a relationship in which God would indeed be God, but would be known as that God who is loving and gracious and forgiving. God had to be in culture to become human. The quest in African Independent Churches and in popular African Christianity is for a Christ who is born of their flesh, a Christ whom they can claim as one of them, and in that way claim him as one of their ancestors. The question is: what does that Christ look like to African Christians?

Faith sheds light by which one can identify those instruments, symbols and images in one's culture that will give meaning to the Christ-event. Zimbabweans, like all African Christians, have been searching for such images and often spontaneously articulating Christologies that can be claimed to be indigenously African. Theologians have also been reflecting on some of the Christological formulations that emerge in popular African Christianity; and we turn now to an exploration of how Christ has been understood within the context of the religious beliefs and practices of the Africans, what salvation means in traditional culture and how Christ can be understood as Saviour of the African world.

NOTES

[1] Some writers prefer the term "African-Instituted Churches". Many studies have been published on this phenomenon throughout Africa. Our treatment in this chapter draws especially on the extensive research by M.L. Daneel into independent churches in Zimbabwe; cf. *Old and New in Southern Shona Independent Churches*, The Hague, Mouton, Vol. 1, *Background and Rise of the Major Movements*, 1971; Vol. 2, *Church Growth — Causative Factors and Recruitment Techniques*, 1974; *The Quest for Belonging*, Gweru, Mambo Press, 1987. See also D.B. Barrett, *Schism and Renewal in Africa*, Nairobi, Addis Ababa and Lusaka, Oxford UP, 1968, pp.96-160.

[2] Daneel, *The Quest for Belonging*, p.46.

[3] J.V. Taylor, *Primal Vision: Christian Presence amid African Religion*, London, SCM, 1963, p.24.
[4] Cited by Basil Davidson, "The Bible and the Gun", in his video series on Africa, distributed by ARM Home Vision.
[5] Cited by M.L. Daneel, "The Growth and Significance of Shona Independent Churches", in M.F.C. Bourdillon, SJ, ed., *Christianity South of the Zambezi*, Vol. 2.
[6] *Ibid.*
[7] Plangger, "Human Rights: A Motive for Mission", *loc. cit.*, p.446.
[8] R.P. Hatendi, "Shona Marriages and the Christian Churches", *loc. cit.*, p.148.
[9] M.F.C. Bourdillon, *The Shona Peoples: An Ethnography of the Contemporary Shona, with Special Reference to their Religion*, Gweru, Mambo Press, 1987, pp.294f.
[10] *Ibid.*, p.297.

6. *Christ, Culture and Salvation*

The essence of the gospel is Jesus Christ, the Son of God and Saviour of the world. But as we read through the New Testament and other early Christian literature, we discover that people tend to understand the gospel in terms of what they already know. Hence, different perceptions of Christ already appeared in early Christianity. One can expect the same variety to characterize African responses to the preaching of the gospel. Does the proclamation of Christ as Saviour in Zimbabwe today meet the yearnings of the people? In this chapter we shall look at some African theological perceptions of salvation which are rooted in the traditional cultures of the people of Zimbabwe and other African peoples.

The yearning for salvation is universal, and peoples everywhere have ways of explaining and coping with evil, sin and suffering. The African life has its joys and sorrows. The effects of sin bring suffering on the family and community. At the same time there is the suffering caused by unpredictable weather patterns, sometimes bringing droughts, sometimes floods, leaving hunger and starvation, sickness and death in their wake. Moreover, the fear of witches and other negative forces is part of the African experience.

African traditionalists believe these negative elements are caused by individuals, either living or the living dead, who manipulate the power God shares with his creatures to produce negative and destructive results. Evil is not seen as caused by a single Satanic figure — at least there is no such idea in any of the Zimbabwean traditional religions with which I am familiar — but by angry ancestors or other spirits, witches or sorcerers. When Africans suffer misfortune they look for the causes in the invisible, which overlaps with the visible to form one world. If a member of the family falls sick or a child dies, there must be a cause and that cause is invariably traced to either an angry ancestor spirit or a wicked spirit operating through a witch. Hence a diviner must be consulted. Even if a doctor establishes that a person has died of cancer or AIDS or some other incurable disease, the traditionalist will want to know why the guardian spirits of the deceased allowed that particular disease to cause that death or to inflict so much pain and suffering. Any failures, disappointments and frustrations in life are similarly attributed to some hostile force and seen as indicating that the guardian spirits have turned their backs on the family.

The traditional perception of salvation must be understood from the perspective of the overlap and interaction between the physical and spiritual worlds, the visible and the invisible. This worldview defines time in cyclical terms, with a future which is not too distant and which is primarily thought of in terms of the present that one experiences and the past one knows to exist because it has been experienced.[1] The world of the ancestors is the future world to which all go when they die, but it is not removed from the present world. In death one moves as it were into the past in order to live in the present as an invisible member of society, to be remembered and to be allowed to participate in the life of the community. The idea of a heaven and a hell still to come in the future is inconceivable in terms of African traditional thought. Salvation can, therefore, only be thought of in terms of being saved from the problems, hardships, misfortunes, injustices, sicknesses and death which people experience in this world.[2] To be saved means living a blissful life on earth. That life, however, can only be life in community, and that salvation can only be real if it is salvation of the whole community and not just the individual.

Since there is always a link between sin and salvation in the preaching of the gospel, it is necessary to enquire into the African understanding of sin in order to be able to translate the gospel message of salvation. How is the whole community involved, for example, in the suffering that comes as a result of a sin committed by an individual member of a family? How is sin itself understood? According to the New Testament, sin brings death, and salvation means receiving that free gift of God which is eternal life through faith in Jesus Christ (cf. Rom. 6:22f.). The Son of God was sent by the Father to be "the atoning sacrifice for our sins" (1 John 4:10).

Sin and salvation in African traditional religions have to do with the life of both the individual and the community because life for African peoples is meaningful only in community, in the extended family community. There is a communal responsibility for the behaviour of every member of the community. The African family is always extended and is made up of the living and their living dead (ancestors), whose presence is very much felt. Parents cannot separate themselves from their children, grandchildren and great-grandchildren. The whole family must always remain together. As children grow up and marry, they should not leave their parents to build their own homes away from them, but remain within the same *kraal* or village in which they live, eating, playing and working together with fathers and mothers, grandfathers and grandmothers, uncles and aunts, nephews and nieces and cousins, essentially looking after one another. One cannot conceive of a happy life apart from one's family: as Riana the Luo traditional diviner put it, "the good life is with and among people, your own people".[3] One must share in the joys and frustrations of the family — its curses and blessings, successes and failures, salvation or condemnation, hopes and aspirations — and in its religious beliefs and practices, since religion is identical with and inseparable from life itself.

It follows that any attempt to define sin and salvation as purely "an individualistic unburdening of personal sin by what has happened to Jesus Christ on the cross"[4] is bound to have a negative effect on the African traditional communal perception of life together — which I believe is also at the heart of the biblical message.

The strong communal or family ties extend beyond the clan to the tribe, which is seen as having a common ancestry whose lineage is perpetuated in the chief's house. Hence the chief is seen as the father of all his subjects. Moreover, all of humanity is believed to have been created by God, which means that all people share in the parenthood of God, which brings them into a single family of God. Sin may therefore affect not only the individual committing it but also the whole community or the entire family of God. An evil action has consequences for one's relationship with God and with the rest of the family, including the living departed elders.

Traditional societies understand sin as any action violating the integrity of God's creation, disrupting relationships within the family and community as a whole and bringing suffering or even death. A sinful action may deprive the individual and his or her community of peace, happiness, wellness and prosperity. Repentance must therefore involve the whole community and not just the individual.

The Shona belief in the *ngozi* spirit (spirit of vengeance) is a clear illustration of this. A *ngozi* is the spirit of a member of the family who died aggrieved or was murdered, which can return and kill relatives of the individual responsible until the crime has been confessed and compensation made to the members of the family of the deceased. A family that feels it has been sinned against by another family may also raise the spirit of one of its deceased members to come as a *ngozi* and kill members of the other family until they acknowledge their sin and make compensation. Failure to care for one's parents is sin against them and the ancestors, who will get angry and bring misfortune or withhold blessings; and when the parents die they too may bring a curse on their descendants by maltreating them during their last days in this world. Ignoring one's ancestors is sin against them, and the whole extended family, including their cattle, goats and sheep and crops in the fields, may be affected because of the action of the one member of the family.

Another clear example is incest, which defiles the extended family and tribe. It is so grave that it affects all of God's creation. Rains are withheld as punishment, leading to severe drought, with all the consequences this has for a people who depend on cattle and farming for their livelihood.

In a traditional African context, Maimela observes, sin is primarily an offense against one's neighbour, a denial of that which makes communal fellowship and stability possible.[5] In other words, one actually sins against God by sinning against one's neighbour. The emphasis is on relationships here and now, but those relationships ultimately affect one's relation to God and the living dead, who then cease to offer protection to the sinner and the members of his or her family. God and the ancestors can never be on the side of the sinner until the sinner comes to deal justly with others in the community.

As far as the traditionalist is concerned, sin cannot be understood in terms of a theology of original sin. Rather, it is seen in terms of concrete deeds by an individual or family, either deliberately or unknowingly, against a neighbour or another family and thus affecting relationships and the well-being of the individual, the family and the community, and creation as a whole.

Within a traditional African context, then, how can we move from this corporate responsibility for sin to individual responsibility? It is important not to destroy the unity of the community. The concept of the body of Christ makes all Christians, as members of the one body, responsible for one another. When one member suffers all suffer, in joy all rejoice. This extends to corporate responsibility for a member's sin, which defiles the whole body of Christ. Christians cannot rejoice with a member who is in sin, and there is great joy in the whole body of Christ when a sinner repents.

Since African thought is not given to speculation but rather thinks in terms of concrete, experienced life situations, salvation must be something people experience in this world here and now, not in some future world after the resurrection, and if there is a hell it must also belong to the world of experience. Indeed, the African lives in a very hostile world.[6]

Since sin affects the whole community including innocent children, animals and other creatures, salvation must therefore involve a series of ritual acts intended to protect and to save the individual from the moment of conception in the mother's womb until death. But the salvation of the individual also means the salvation of the whole family and community. As soon as conception has taken place, the life of the mother and the child are threatened by hostile powers; and protective medicine must be used immediately. The rites of passage must be performed to save the individual and the family from hostile forces at birth, puberty, marriage and death, which are critical moments in the life of the community. Because they mark a transition from one stage of life to another, action must be taken to ensure that this goes smoothly and the family is saved.

While the birth of a child is an opportunity to celebrate the gift of life, it is also filled with anxiety because misfortune at that point may affect the family's lineage. Any action which then saves the family from extinction by allowing its life to be perpetuated through that child is salvific. The ancestors are also saved from annihilation, for not having a descendant among the living to remember you after you are dead is like being non-existent. The family priest presides over rituals and sacrifices directed to the ancestral spirits, and through them to God, requesting salvation, protection from witches and other malevolent powers and a life of peace, happiness and prosperity on earth.[7]

With this understanding of salvation as abundant life, traditionalists spend much time seeking protection through diviners, making sacrifices and pleading for a blissful life. If the gospel is to be relevant and meaningful in this context it must point not only to a life of happiness in the future but also to a meaningful life in this world. Motivated by the gospel message, the church must engage in activities that aim to improve the quality of the life of the people and must see those activities as an integral part of its proclamation of Christ. The struggle against poverty, ignorance, disease and oppression is a means through which Christ's saving power is manifest here and now. Through these visible acts of salvation Christ is seen to be saving the world. While the church cannot avoid pointing to the future fulfilment — for despite all our efforts to change this world, imperfection, sin, death and suffering continue — the preaching of a future salvation alone will not suffice in an African context.

This commitment to improve the quality of the life of the African people has in many respects made the gospel relevant as an instrument for social transformation and has made the church acceptable as a partner in nation-building. The kingdom of God is about a new people, a new society, a new culture. Through the preaching of the gospel, the church works to bring about this new society, not through the imposition of foreign cultures but through an internal transformation coming as a result of the gospel working within the individual and the community as a whole.

The kingdom of God is both an already and a not yet, a present and an eschatological reality. It begins in this world as communities are led by the gospel to transform themselves and their cultures so that they are indeed seen to be a new people created in the image of God. When the church cooperates with secular institutions to improve the quality of life for all, it is participating in a divinely constituted process which is essential to its ministry and can only lead to the manifestation of the kingdom of God. The state of being saved begins here and now; it means having life and having it abundantly. Salvation, therefore, from a Christian traditionalist's perspective must offer protection and deliverance from the suffering and misery of this world. It means living a life of wellness and prosperity and being able to live with Christ and your ancestors upon death.

How then can Christ be seen as saviour of the African world? What perceptions of Christ have emerged in popular African Christianity and express an African cultural ethos? In the light of the traditional worldview which continues to be a part of the vast majority of the African people in Zimbabwe, as in most of Africa, both in the rural and urban centres, how are the person and work of Christ understood? Which images of Christ speak directly to the African context? How do Africans within that context deal with the conflict that is bound to emerge in the encounter with the gospel?

As people everywhere tend to understand the gospel in terms of what they already know, one image that has become christologically relevant to the ordinary African is that of the ancestor. It is not unusual for traditionalists to argue that Christ must be seen as an ancestor, a departed elder, since he is proclaimed as an intermediary between God and humanity. According to traditional religions, each family or clan relates to God only through its own departed elders, and it is inconceivable that one should turn to the departed elders of families with whom one has no blood relationship. Some African traditionalists have thus argued that Christ must be understood as one among many departed elders, and should therefore relate specifically to the Jewish people or, more broadly, to white people. Others, who have become Christians but continue to feel some attachment to traditional religious beliefs and practices, would argue that while departed elders continue to function as intermediaries, Christ must be understood as the most senior of the living departed elders, the apex of the pyramid of all intermediaries, above whom there is only God. Christ is therefore seen as universal, interceding for all of humanity. As the only begotten Son of God, he is related to all of humankind. His blood makes all persons blood relatives, and he must therefore be seen as a "brother" ancestor.[8]

The "departed elder" or "ancestral spirit" Christology represents a genuine African effort to understand the life and work of Christ, drawing on what God has already revealed to them about their relationship with him. Such an exercise is bound to result in different Christological perceptions — as happened in early Christianity, when different Christologies emerged, some of which, popular though they were with certain groups, were later rejected as heresy.[9] People everywhere tend to understand new reality in terms of what they already know, and in that process there are bound to be many syncretistic tendencies. But where there is a serious engagement between gospel and culture, it is bound also to be creative and to produce new theological insights. The "departed elder" Christologies seek to resolve the conflict between the Christian proclamation of the gospel message in Africa and the indigenous cultures of the African people.

When theological reflection within an African context draws from the numerous symbols and images in African cultures, the gospel with its power can transform those cultures from within, so that the people indeed become people as God wants them to be. Our experience in Zimbabwe is that the worldview of African cultures and religions cannot easily be brushed aside if Christian preaching about salvation through faith in Jesus Christ is to be relevant.[10] When the gospel genuinely enters into a people's culture, it permeates all aspects of that culture, creating a new understanding, new relationships and a new mission. In Zimbabwe, the need is to allow the gospel to have an impact on ritual action as it relates to the communion with the living dead, which is an integral aspect of traditional belief and ritual. Given the freedom to operate on its own, the gospel of Christ will create within our African cultures new ways of relating to the departed members of the family.

The rituals which are performed at every important stage of one's life in traditional societies emphasize the sanctity of life as a whole. The gospel should sanctify all of culture and affirm that sanctity sacramentally on different occasions in the life of believers. Since ritual action is so important to African traditional religions, it is essential for African Christians to define for themselves, in the light of the gospel, their understanding of sacraments. Transformation, and not rejection, of traditional rituals can contribute significantly to creating a new culture and a new people, able to commit themselves totally to a life inspired by the values proclaimed through the preaching of Christ.

To sum up, African life can be meaningful only as life in community. The community shares in the joys and sorrows of the individual and is affected by the misconduct of any member of the family or clan. Life is meaningful only if it is a life of sharing with fellow human beings, with the whole of God's creation, with the living dead, and through them with God. There is therefore a bond of unity among all the people of this world as well as with the spirit world. This means that in terms of African thought, "when one member suffers all suffer". Salvation must be comprehensive, holistic, embracing all aspects of human existence and its environment.

We have seen that the concepts of sin and salvation are already present within the African traditional religious context. The task of African Christian theology is to bring Christ into this context and make him the centre of all talk about sin and salvation. Christ has borne the sins not only of the individual but also of the community of believers. Christian concern for one another makes salvation a present reality. Christ as ancestor makes the Christian look forward to his or her own elevation to the status of ancestor together with Christ, which is a resurrection to a position of power.

Christianity has been successfully planted in Zimbabwe and is growing very rapidly. As the African peoples in their different situations try to live out their Christian faith, conflict is inevitable, for they will hear the gospel challenging their worldview and their social, economic, religious and political environment. In such conflict situations, new theologies are bound to emerge as various groups seek to appropriate the Christian faith and practice within their own context. It is therefore within the context of the relationship between gospel and culture that the emergence of new Christological perspectives and perceptions must be seen.

NOTES

[1] For an extensive discussion of the African concept of time, see J.S. Mbiti, *African Religions and Philosophy*, New York, Praeger, 1969.

[2] This section draws on the stimulating discussion by S.S. Maimela, "Salvation in African Traditional Religion", *Missionalia*, Vol. 13, No. 2, 1985, pp.63-77.

[3] Michael C. Kirwen, *The Missionary and the Diviner: Contending Theologies of Christian and African Religions*, Maryknoll, NY, Orbis, 1987, p.76.

[4] S.S. Maimela, *op. cit.*, p.66.

[5] *Ibid.*, p.74. In an earlier, unpublished version of this article, Maimela expressed the same idea much more pointedly by defining sin in African Traditional Religions as something understood "more in terms of a breach of fellowship with our neighbours that manifests itself through a state of absence of brotherhood and sisterhood — that is, lack of love in communal relationships — than in terms of divine retributive law which must be obeyed and whose justice must be satisfied by human beings in their relationships with God".

[6] Cf. H. Sawyer, "Sin and Salvation: Soteriology Viewed from the African Situation", in Becken, ed., *Relevant Theology for Africa*, Durban, Lutheran Publishing House, 1973, p.129.

[7] On salvation in other African traditional religions see C. Gaba, "Man's Salvation in African Traditional Religion", in E. Fashole-Luke et al., eds, *Christianity in Independent Africa*, pp.389-401.

[8] Cf. Charles Nyamiti, *Christ As Our Ancestor: Christology from an African Perspective*, Gweru, Mambo Press, 1984; see also J.S. Pobee, *Towards an African Theology*, Nashville, Abingdon Press, 1979.

[9] Cf. Walter Bauer, *Orthodoxy and Heresy in Earliest Christianity*, Philadelphia, Fortress, 1971; James Robinson and Helmut Koester, *Trajectories through Early Christianity*, Philadelphia, Fortress, 1971.

[10] Cf. my article "An African Lutheran Theology", in Albert Pero and Ambrose Moyo, eds, *Theology and the Black Experience: The Lutheran Heritage Interpreted by African and African-American Theologians*, Minneapolis, Augsburg, 1988, pp.92f.

7. *The Risk of Incarnation*

Wherever the gospel is preached, the gospel and culture question is unavoidable, because the proclamation of the gospel involves crossing cultural and religious boundaries with the same message. The gospel takes place in the encounter between Christ and the individual person within his or her specific cultural milieu, and it is in and through the preaching of the church that the encounter is made possible. But that gospel to become gospel must be heard (Rom. 10) in order to produce a response. Both the hearing and the response are possible only in and through culture. Culture provides the ears with which one hears the gospel as well as the eyes with which one sees Christ.[1]

In view of the negative attitude of the mainline churches towards the indigenous cultures of the people of Zimbabwe, which is still prevalent, and the insistence of many Zimbabwean Christians on retaining a great deal of their traditional cultures, the church is being challenged to be open to other religious traditions rooted in our traditional cultures and to capture the images and symbols that can effectively proclaim the gospel.

The gospel cannot be preached apart from the culture of the people to whom it is being proclaimed because in the first place it must be communicated through the cultural media. But this unavoidable link with culture is also because the gospel concerns the incarnation, God's becoming a human being, being born in history, in a particular culture, and thus communicating with human beings at their level, which is the level of culture. Jesus was a Jew and remained a Jew until his death, fulfilling all Jewish customs, including burial "according to the burial custom of the Jews" (John 19:40). Jewish scholars insist that within Judaism religion and ethics cannot be abstracted from the rest of life: it "is not only religion and it is not only ethics: it is the sum total of all needs of the nation, placed on a religious basis... Judaism is a national life, a life which the national religion and human ethical principles embrace without engulfing."[2] The message of Jesus aimed to make an impact on the whole of Jewish life since Judaism as a religion practised by Jesus' contemporaries was part and parcel of Jewish culture. Any challenge to their religious beliefs and practices was understood as a challenge to their culture as whole. The social, economic and political systems had a religious base and to challenge that base was to challenge the entire structure. Jesus did not reject their religion, but affirmed its spirit and went on to challenge the whole religious structure to be faithful to its calling as an instrument of God's love. In the midst of African traditional religions, which already had some knowledge of God, Christ challenges those religions and cultures to renew themselves in the light of God's self-revelation so that they too may declare the glory of God as they are renewed from within. All this represents a threat to those who wield religious or political power. Because Jesus worked from within Judaism, he was seen as a threat to Jewish culture and to their survival as a people. In that same sense the gospel must be indeed a threat to African culture and African religions in Zimbabwe, but it also brings new hope and a new people — created in the image of God, not in the image of the European missionary.

As Jesus spoke from within Jewish culture, of which he was a product and a part, and as he sought to relate the whole of Jewish life and culture to the Godhead, his interests and his priorities were contrary to the expectations of his Jewish counterparts. He evoked resentment by being unafraid to challenge acceptable cultural values which he believed to be contrary to the will of God. He sought to transform it with his message of love. Jesus took upon himself a human form in order to transform humanity and create a new person out of the old. A new culture can therefore only be created from the old.

The incarnation was indeed a great risk, which God took in order to communicate his love for the world. That risk must be repeated wherever the gospel of Christ is proclaimed. This means allowing the gospel to die in culture in order that it may bring to life with itself a new culture and a new people. Christian missions in Zimbabwe have tended to see African traditional beliefs and practices as pollution, from which the gospel needs to be protected. The message of the resurrection challenges the church to recognize God's power in bringing to life that which is inseparably bound to him. The gospel should enter into culture with God's power, die in culture and, with God's power and the assurance of resurrection, enliven the whole of a people's culture with that message of God's love. Only when the church has allowed the gospel to enter into Zimbabwean culture and die in that culture can one speak of an inseparable relationship between gospel and culture. There are signs of this happening in Zimbabwean Christianity, but Christians need to reflect together and allow the Spirit to lead them towards the new life and new culture with Christ and in Christ.

NOTES

[1] A helpful survey of ecumenical discussion of this issue and a theoretical framework for responding to it in specific contexts are offered by S. Wesley Ariarajah, *Gospel and Culture: An Ongoing Discussion Within the Ecumenical Movement*, Geneva, WCC, 1994.

[2] Niebuhr, *Christ and Culture*, p.3.